CHICAGO

CHICAGO **ARCHITECTURE** FOUNDATION

Pomegranate

SAN FRANCISCO

Pomegranate Communications, Inc.
Box 808022, Petaluma, California 94975
800-227-1428
www.pomegranate.com

Pomegranate Europe Ltd.
Unit 1, Heathcote Business Centre, Hurlbutt Road
Warwick, Warwickshire CV34 6TD, UK
[+44] 0 1926 430111; sales@pomeurope.co.uk

ISBN 978-0-7649-2586-3
Pomegranate Catalog No. AA229

Pomegranate publishes books of
postcards on a wide range of subjects.
Please contact the publisher for more information.

Cover designed by Gina Bostian
Printed in Korea
14 13 12 11 10 09 08 07 06   11 10 9 8 7 6 5 4 3

To facilitate detachment of the postcards from this book, fold each card along its perforation line before tearing.

The Chicago Architecture Foundation has, since its founding in 1966, played an important role in promoting public awareness and appreciation of Chicago's architectural treasures. Along with the Foundation's popular walking, bike, and bus tours, its river cruises are a great way for both visitors and residents to learn about the city's development, the origins and construction of its world-class buildings, the visionaries who designed these structures, and the stylistic influences—from Beaux-Arts and the Chicago School to Art Deco and Postmodernism—that characterize Chicago architecture. For more information about these tours, visit the Foundation's website, www.architecture.org.

Many of the superb images in this collection are from the book *A View from the River: The Chicago Architecture Foundation River Cruise* (Pomegranate, 2000); all are the work of the respected architectural photography house Hedrich Blessing. More views of famous Chicago landmarks—including interior shots and rare historical photographs—can be found in Pomegranate's series of Building Books, also published in cooperation with the Chicago Architecture Foundation: *Marshall Field's, Sears Tower, The Reliance Building, The Rookery, The Auditorium Building,* and *The Merchandise Mart.*

CHICAGO

Swissôtel, 1989
Architects: Harry Weese and Associates
Photograph by Marco Lorenzetti © Hedrich Blessing

BOX 808022 PETALUMA CA 94975

Pomegranate

CHICAGO

Wrigley Building (left), 1921–1924
Architects: Graham, Anderson, Probst & White
Tribune Tower, 1925
Architects: Howells & Hood
Photograph by Scott McDonald © Hedrich Blessing

BOX 808022 PETALUMA CA 94975

Pomegranate

CHICAGO

333 North Michigan Avenue (left), 1928
Architects: Holabird & Root
London Guarantee and Accident Building, 1923
Architect: Alfred S. Alschuler
Photograph by Jon Miller © Hedrich Blessing

BOX 808022   PETALUMA   CA 94975

Pomegranate

CHICAGO

333 West Wacker Drive, 1983
Architects: Kohn Pedersen Fox
Photograph by Bob Harr © Hedrich Blessing

BOX 808022   PETALUMA   CA 94975

Pomegranate

CHICAGO

860–880 North Lake Shore Drive, 1949–1951
Architect: Ludwig Mies van der Rohe
Photograph © Hedrich Blessing

BOX 808022 PETALUMA CA 94975

Pomegranate

CHICAGO

Aon Center, 1973
Architects: Edward Durrell Stone with Perkins & Will
Photograph by Scott McDonald © Hedrich Blessing

BOX 808022   PETALUMA   CA 94975

Pomegranate

CHICAGO

Boeing World Headquarters, 1990
Architects: Perkins & Will
Photograph by Nick Merrick © Hedrich Blessing

BOX 808022   PETALUMA   CA 94975

Pomegranate

CHICAGO

Carson Pirie Scott & Company, 1904
Architect: Louis H. Sullivan
Addition: D. H. Burnham & Company, 1906
Photography by Jon Miller © Hedrich Blessing

BOX 808022   PETALUMA   CA 94975

Pomegranate

CHICAGO

Chicago Skyline
Photograph by Bob Shimer © Hedrich Blessing

BOX 808022   PETALUMA   CA 94975

Pomegranate

CHICAGO

Chicago Sun-Times Building (front left), 1957
Architects: Naess & Murphy
Photograph by Bob Shimer © Hedrich Blessing

BOX 808022   PETALUMA   CA 94975

Pomegranate

CHICAGO

Citicorp Center, 1987
Architects: Murphy/Jahn
Photograph by Scott McDonald © Hedrich Blessing

BOX 808022   PETALUMA   CA 94975

Pomegranate

CHICAGO

City of Bridges
Photograph by Bob Harr © Hedrich Blessing

BOX 808022   PETALUMA   CA 94975

Pomegranate

© CHICAGO **ARCHITECTURE** FOUNDATION
A portion of the proceeds from the sale of this postcard helps to support
CAF education programs.

CHICAGO

Daily News Building, 1929
Architects: Holabird & Root
Photograph by Bob Shimer © Hedrich Blessing

BOX 808022   PETALUMA   CA 94975

Pomegranate

CHICAGO

Hyatt Regency Hotel (front center, with towers behind and
to the right), 1974–1980
Architects: A. Epstein and Sons
Photograph by Bob Shimer © Hedrich Blessing

BOX 808022   PETALUMA   CA 94975

Pomegranate

CHICAGO

Inland Steel Building, *1954–1958*
Architects: Skidmore, Owings & Merrill
Photograph by Nick Merrick © Hedrich Blessing

BOX 808022   PETALUMA   CA 94975

Pomegranate

CHICAGO

Jewelers Building (left), 1926
Architects: Giaver & Dinkelberg with Thielbar & Fugard
United of America Building, 1962
Architects: Shaw, Metz & Associates
Photograph by Geoff Nicholson © Hedrich Blessing

BOX 808022   PETALUMA   CA 94975

Pomegranate

CHICAGO

John Hancock Center, 1969
Architects: Skidmore, Owings & Merrill
Photograph by Jon Miller © Hedrich Blessing

BOX 808022   PETALUMA   CA 94975

Pomegranate

CHICAGO

Marina City (twin towers), 1967
Architects: Bertrand Goldberg Associates
IBM Building, 1971
Architects: Office of Mies van der Rohe with C. F. Murphy
Associates
Photograph by Geoff Nicholson © Hedrich Blessing

BOX 808022   PETALUMA   CA 94975

Pomegranate

CHICAGO

Merchandise Mart, 1930
Architects: Graham, Anderson, Probst & White
Photograph by Bob Shimer © Hedrich Blessing

BOX 808022 PETALUMA CA 94975

Pomegranate

CHICAGO

One Illinois Center (second from right), 1970
Architects: Office of Mies van der Rohe
333 North Michigan Avenue (right), 1928
Architects: Holabird & Root
Photograph by Scott McDonald © Hedrich Blessing

BOX 808022   PETALUMA   CA 94975

Pomegranate

CHICAGO

NBC Tower, *1989*
Architects: Skidmore, Owings & Merrill
Photograph by Nick Merrick © Hedrich Blessing

BOX 808022   PETALUMA   CA 94975

Pomegranate

CHICAGO

The North Bank
Photograph by Bob Harr © Hedrich Blessing

BOX 808022   PETALUMA   CA 94975

Pomegranate

CHICAGO

Quaker Tower (glass-walled building, center), **Westin River North Hotel** (next building, right), and **Marina City** (twin towers)
Photograph by Bob Shimer © Hedrich Blessing

BOX 808022   PETALUMA   CA 94975

Pomegranate

© CHICAGO ARCHITECTURE FOUNDATION
A portion of the proceeds from the sale of this postcard helps to support CAF education programs.

CHICAGO

R. R. Donnelley Center, 1992
Architects: Ricardo Bofill Arquitectura with DeStefano &
Partners
Photograph by Marco Lorenzetti © Hedrich Blessing

BOX 808022 PETALUMA CA 94975

Pomegranate

CHICAGO

Reliance Building, 1895
Architects: D. H. Burnham & Company
Photograph by Craig Dugan of Hedrich Blessing,
courtesy McClier

BOX 808022   PETALUMA   CA 94975

Pomegranate

CHICAGO

River City, 1986
Architects: Bertrand Goldberg Associates
Photograph by Geoff Nicholson © Hedrich Blessing

BOX 808022   PETALUMA   CA 94975

Pomegranate

CHICAGO

Sears Tower, 1974
Architects: Skidmore, Owings & Merrill
Photograph by Bob Nick © Hedrich Blessing

BOX 808022   PETALUMA   CA 94975

Pomegranate

CHICAGO

Swissôtel, 1989
Architects: Harry Weese and Associates
Photograph by Marco Lorenzetti © Hedrich Blessing

BOX 808022   PETALUMA   CA 94975

Pomegranate

CHICAGO

Wrigley Building, 1921–1924
Architects: Graham, Anderson, Probst & White
Photograph by Marco Lorenzetti © Hedrich Blessing

BOX 808022   PETALUMA   CA 94975

Pomegranate

CHICAGO

333 West Wacker Drive, 1983
Architects: Kohn Pedersen Fox
Photograph by Bob Harr © Hedrich Blessing

BOX 808022   PETALUMA   CA 94975

Pomegranate

Selected Pomegranate Books of Postcards on Architecture and Design

Please contact Pomegranate for more information about our many books of postcards.

Chicago rebounded from its famous fire of 1871 with an onslaught of construction. In 1885 the city celebrated the completion of the first skyscraper—the nine-story Home Insurance Building—initiating a new e in architecture and marking Chicago as the world's center of the skyscra a distinction that it holds to this day. Driven by the talents and vision of such trailblazing architects as Louis Sullivan, D. H. Burnham, and John Wellborn Root, and in succeeding decades by former Bauhaus director Ludwig Mies van der Rohe and the megafirm Skidmore, Owings & Mer (among others), Chicago has sustained its tradition of innovative enginee and dramatic design.

This book of postcards presents thirty views of Chicago's remarkabl buildings and skyline by Hedrich Blessing photographers.

CHICAGO **ARCHITECTURE** FOUNDATION

$9.95 ($13.95 CAN.)

Pomegranate

ISBN 978-0-7649-2

CATALOG No. AA229

9 780764 925863

7 17195 20239 2

CONTAINS THIRTY OVERSIZED POSTCARDS